We are
MUSLIMS

Philip Blake

W
FRANKLIN WATTS
LONDON • SYDNEY

This edition copyright © Franklin Watts 2015

Franklin Watts
338 Euston Road
London, NW1 3BH

Franklin Watts Australia
Level 17/207 Kent Street
Sydney, NSW 2000

Series designed and created for Franklin Watts by Storeybooks.

Acknowledgements
The Publisher would like to thank Jasmine, Jeffrey, Mohammad and Serish
for their help in producing this book.
Faith advisor Sahrukh Husain

Photo credits:
Georgios Kollidas/Dreasmtime: front cover bl. Witthayap/Dreamstime: front
cover br. Aamir Qureshi/AFP/Getty Images; I Stock pp 4, 5, 9, 11, 12, 19, 21
and 25; Tudor Photography pp 1(right), 3(bottom right), 6(bottom) 20 and
31; Every attempt has been made to clear copyright. Should there be any
inadvertent omission please apply to the publisher for rectification.

Additional photographs were supplied by the children featured in the book.

Dewey number: 294.3

ISBN: 978 1 4451 3888 6

Printed in Malaysia

Franklin Watts is a division of Hachette Children's Books,
an Hachette UK company. www.hachette.co.uk

Note:
The opinions expressed in this book are personal to the children
we talked to and all opinions are subjective and can vary.

Contents

Words in **bold** can be found in the glossary.

What is Islam?

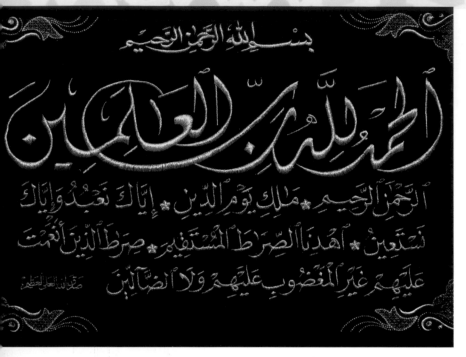

Followers of Islam, who are known as Muslims, believe that there is one God, who is called Allah, and that Muhammad (pbuh) is his messenger. Their beliefs are set down in the Qur'an, which they believe contains the words of God as revealed to Muhammad (pbuh).

▲ One of the arts for which Islam is famous is calligraphy, the art of beautiful writing. Verses from the Qur'an are written or embroidered in an elegant, flowing script.

Talking about the Prophet
Muhammad is the prophet of Islam, so Muslims are always very respectful when they speak about him. They often use the phrase 'peace be upon him' when referring to him by name, and in writing is it common to shorten this to '**pbuh**'.

The Prophet Muhammad (pbuh)
Muhammad (pbuh) lived from about CE 570 to 632 and was the prophet of Islam. He was given the task of spreading the message that is now contained in the Qur'an. A brave and intelligent man, he led the first Muslim **community**, and stayed true to his beliefs in spite of opposition.

The early Muslims
The first Muslims lived in the Arabian Peninsula, in what is now Saudi Arabia. Muhammad (pbuh) was born and grew up in the city of Makka, but was

▲ *This **mosque** is at Medina, Saudi Arabia, a city where Muhammad (pbuh) lived.*

persecuted there for his beliefs, so the people of Yathrib (now Medina) invited him and his followers to live there. Later he defeated the non-believers at Makka, so Islam flourished in both cities.

The Five Pillars

Muslims observe five key requirements of their faith, which are known as the Five **Pillars** of Islam (see pages 8–9). The Pillars are **Shahada** (the **profession** of faith), **Salaat** (regular prayer), fasting during the month of **Ramadan**, **Zakat** (the payment of money to help the poor), and **Hajj** (the pilgrimage to the holy city of Makka).

At mosques people leave their shoes near the entrance before going in to pray. ▶

Islam Around the World

From its base in the Arabian Peninsula, Islam spread rapidly through the Middle East, western Asia and North Africa in the centuries after the lifetime of Muhammad (pbuh). Traders, soldiers and scholars carried news of the faith around the world and Muslim communities grew in many countries.

The spread of Islam

Today, most of the countries of the Middle East are Muslim, together with Iran, Indonesia, Pakistan and most of the countries of North Africa. As well as these Muslim nations, there are many countries, such as Britain and India, that are home to many Muslims. As their populations increase, and as Muslims all over the world encourage others to adopt their beliefs, the size of the worldwide Islamic population is growing and there are now at least 1.2 billion Muslims in the world.

My name is Jasmine Zonneveld. I live in Los Angeles, USA, but my mom is Malaysian and my dad is Dutch. I am an only child. I go to a public school in Los Angeles and I like soccer, running, hiking and spending time with my family.

I am Serish. I live in Banbury, England and I am nine years old. I have one sister and three brothers and I like ice skating and shopping.

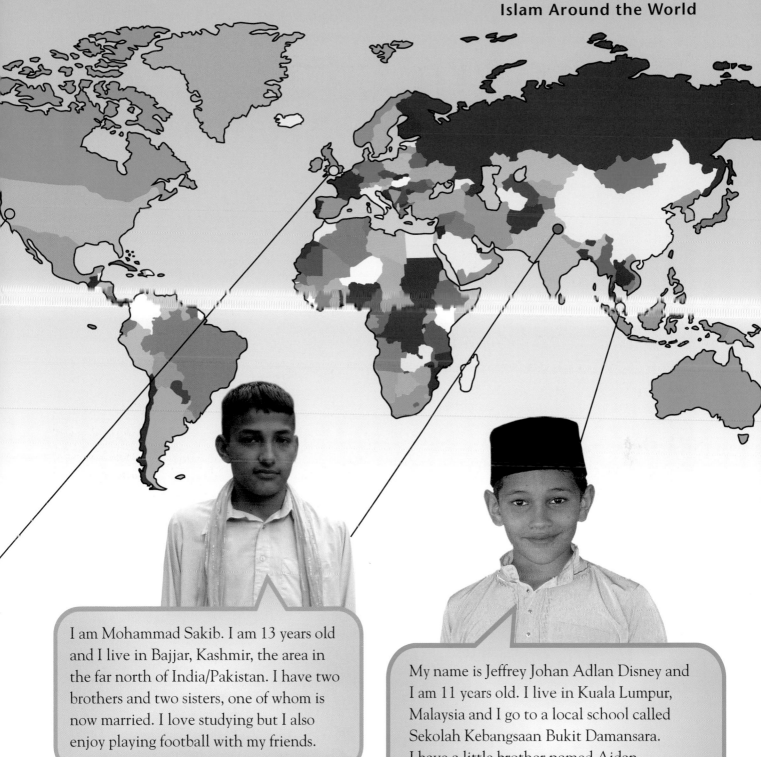

I am Mohammad Sakib. I am 13 years old and I live in Bajjar, Kashmir, the area in the far north of India/Pakistan. I have two brothers and two sisters, one of whom is now married. I love studying but I also enjoy playing football with my friends.

My name is Jeffrey Johan Adlan Disney and I am 11 years old. I live in Kuala Lumpur, Malaysia and I go to a local school called Sekolah Kebangsaan Bukit Damansara. I have a little brother named Aidan Iskandar and a big sister named Yasmin. I love drama, public speaking and acting, just like my sister. Apart from that, I also enjoy gymnastics and swimming.

In this book, four children share their experiences of Islamic faith. It is important to remember that other Muslims will have different opinions and experiences of their own faith.

A Muslim Life
Jeffrey's story

▲ *This is my family. As Muslims, we follow the Five Pillars of Islam.*

Where I live in Malaysia, Islam is the religion of the majority of the population, but there are also many Buddhists, Christians, Hindus and followers of other faiths. We live together peacefully and followers of the different faiths learn from each other. As a Muslim, I follow the Five Pillars of Islam. These Pillars provide a guide for Muslims on what we should do with our lives.

The Profession of Faith

The first Pillar, the Shahada, is the profession of faith: 'There is no God but Allah and Muhammad (pbuh) is his Messenger.' This tells us that there is only one God and that the Prophet Muhammad (pbuh) was the man sent to us by Allah to teach us about the true faith, Islam. The Shahada is what every Muslim must say sincerely to show their belief in Islam. Even if you are born into a Muslim family, you have not properly entered Islam until you have said these words and meant them with all your heart.

The other four Pillars

Salaat means the compulsory prayers five times a day. Fasting during the month of Ramadan involves abstaining from food and water during the daylight hours of this month. The payment of Zakat is the donation of a certain amount of money according to your income to poorer or less fortunate people. The Hajj is the pilgrimage to Makka, to pray in front of the **Ka'aba**. This pilgrimage is not compulsory but every Muslim should do it, unless they are physically unable or do not have enough money to go. In Malaysia, there is a special bank called the *Tabung Hajji* that helps you save money for the Hajj.

Serish says:
We fast during Ramadan so that our sins are forgiven and our bodies are cleansed.

▼ *In countries such as Egypt, Muslims who have been on the Hajj decorate their houses with pictures of the rituals and events that take place on the pilgrimage.*

9

The Qur'an
Jeffrey's story

◄ *When I read the Qur'an I try to concentrate hard and follow the Arabic text with care.*

The sacred book of Islam is called the Qur'an. Its words were revealed to the Prophet Muhammad (pbuh) through the angel Jibril over a period of 23 years. The Prophet Muhammad's (pbuh) followers and scribes memorised the words and, because there was no paper in those days, they wrote the words down on whatever they could find, such as animal skins, leaves and rocks. Later they wrote all the words in one big book, which is now the Qur'an. The words of the Qur'an have been unchanged since that time.

The Arabic language

The Qur'an is written in traditional Arabic. It is important for Muslims to learn Arabic because it helps us to fully understand the true meaning of the Qur'an. Even though the Qur'an has been translated into many different languages so everyone can read it, it is still better to be able to read it in Arabic, the language in which it was revealed.

> *Jasmine says:*
> I read the Qur'an mainly at home. My mom and I think it is most important to understand the Qur'an.

◀ *This copy of the Qur'an is beautifully printed with a richly decorated border around the text.*

Studying the Qur'an

I learn about the Qur'an mainly at school, where I have six lessons of Islamic studies a week. My teacher is an *Ustaz* (religious teacher) who tells us how to properly recite the Qur'an. Besides that, we also learn about the *adab* (etiquette) of being a good Muslim and learn to memorise verses from the Qur'an. I also read the Qur'an at home. Everyone in my family has read the Qur'an. Although we do not all read it every day, we read it during prayers for special occasions, such as when a family member is going away on a long journey or when someone gets married.

At Prayer
Mohammad's story

◄ *This kneeling posture is one of the positions we use during prayer. It shows that as Muslims we are humble before God.*

Prayer is one of the Pillars of Islam, and Muslims pray five times a day, at set times – between first light and sunrise, just after noon, in the late afternoon, after sunset and in the evening. We can pray wherever we are, provided that we have washed and that the place where we pray is clean.

The time for prayers
Where I live we know when it is time to pray because the **Adhan**, or call to prayer, is made from the mosque by a **muezzin**. When we pray, we normally use a prayer mat, which provides a clean surface. We always face the holy city of Makka when we pray.

Words and movements
Before we say our prayers, we say '*B'ismillah i rahman i rahim*'. This means, 'In the name of Allah, the Compassionate, the Merciful.' We then say our prayers, following a set order of words and motions – standing, bowing down, kneeling and sitting. When prayers end at the mosque, we turn to each other and say, 'Assalamualaikum.' This means, 'Peace be upon you.'

12

A Muslim Wedding
Mohammad's story

◄ *This is me with my sister's husband and his friends before he got married.*

When two people from Muslim families get married it is a time of happiness and rejoicing, when both the couple and their two families are brought together. When my sister got married there was a big build-up when the two families discussed the wedding, a quiet ceremony, and a fun celebration afterwards for the two families.

Finding a partner

In Muslim families, marriages are often arranged by the couple's parents, but the bride and groom have to be happy to marry one another. If one of them does not want to marry the other, they and their family can begin the search for a partner again.

Presents and celebrations

When Muslims get married, the groom gives his wife a present of money. This present is called a bride-gift or **mahr**, and the amount to be paid is agreed before the ceremony and is mentioned in the marriage contract. My sister and brother-in-law were also given money by friends and family.

▼ *Watched by witnesses from both families, the bride signs the marriage contract. The groom also signs, but he does so in a separate room.*

◀ *The bride and groom.*

Jeffrey says:
In Malaysia, couples choose their own marriage partners, with approval from their parents. After a formal wedding ceremony, there are many colourful celebrations and Malay customs, such as a ceremony in which the bride and groom are treated as king and queen for a day.

The ceremony

When my sister got married, the ceremony took place at home – this is quite common for a Muslim wedding. My sister wore a traditional wedding gown called a *lenga*. To make her hair soft, our female relatives put oil on it. The **Imam** came from the local mosque and the serious part of the ceremony took place in front of him. There were readings from the Qur'an and the marriage contract was signed – at this point my sister and brother-in-law were properly married.

Celebrations

After the serious part of the ceremony was over, we all enjoyed a big party with music and lots of delicious food. Some of the guests threw dye at the bridal party to make the event even more colourful.

▲ *The parents of the bride with a bowl of pink dye to throw at the bridal party.*

At My Mosque
Jeffrey's story

▲ *We wash under running water before prayers.*

When it is time to pray, the muezzin at the mosque says the Adhan. This is the long, melodic call to prayer, which sounds a bit like a song. A loudspeaker is placed at the top of the mosque so everyone in the neighbourhood can hear the Adhan.

Before entering

Before entering the mosque we must make sure we are clean and free from dirt. There are taps outside the mosque where I wash under running water. There is a set way Muslims must wash. First, I wash my arms, from the hands up to the elbows. Then I wash my face, head and ears three times, before finally washing my feet and legs. I leave my shoes on the racks outside before entering the mosque.

In the mosque
Inside the mosque the floor is carpeted and the wall has lots of framed verses from the Qur'an. There is a little green arrow on the ceiling that points in the direction of Makka, so we know which way to face when praying.

Friday prayers
People go to the mosque throughout the week, but most people go on Fridays for Salaat Juma'ah (Friday Prayers). School finishes early on this day to give the Muslim students time to go to the mosque and pray. Usually my grandfather fetches me from school and we go to the mosque near our house. Afterwards he always takes me for a nice lunch somewhere!

▼ *We all stand facing Makka, ready to begin our prayers.*

Muslim Clothes
Jasmine's story

The Qur'an contains lots of instructions about how Muslims should live. It says that we should be modest in our dress. Women and girls are also told to keep their breasts covered.

My clothes

The clothes I wear are not very different from those worn by non-Muslim people. I wear casual clothes, such as jeans and T-shirts, like most of the other children in my community. The main difference is that I do not wear short shorts or short skirts. At festivals and on special occasions I wear my nicest clothes – sometimes I wear a long, loose-fitting Malaysian costume called a '*Baju kurung*' because of my mom's Malaysian heritage.

> **Sherish says:**
> I sometimes wear a hijab, which covers my head, but women and girls in my community do not wear a veil to cover their faces.

▲ *These are the kind of clothes I normally wear to school.*

> **Mohammad says:**
> In Kashmir many women cover their heads with a scarf and wear long skirts or trousers.

◄ *Some Muslim women wear a scarf that covers the head and neck.*

▼ *In Saudi Arabia (and occasionally in other Muslim communities) women cover their whole body, except for the eyes.*

Other cultures

In some Muslim communities, women and girls cover their hair with a headscarf or cover their whole body except for the eyes, but where I live, very few wear a scarf and no-one covers their face. I think people in different parts of the world have different understandings of Islam, based on their cultural background. I think being honest, kind and thoughtful, and having a good character is more important than the kind of clothes you wear, provided that you dress modestly.

Feasting and Fasting
Serish's story

◀ *I enjoy eating dates after sunset at Ramadan. Even though I am nine years old I fast during the daytime in Ramadan. It is hard to do this, but it's also rewarding.*

The Qur'an lays down some rules about what Muslims are allowed to eat. There is also one time of the year, the month of Ramadan, when our diet changes completely, as we fast. At this time we also concentrate especially hard on our prayers and our religion.

Jeffrey says:
Fasting during Ramadan is the third of the Pillars of Islam. We do not eat or drink during the daylight hours of this month.

Halal or haram

We are forbidden to drink alcohol, and there are also a few foods that Muslims are not allowed to eat. These foods are known as **haram**, whereas foods fit to eat are called **halal**. Pork is haram, but other meats are halal provided that the animals are slaughtered in the proper way.

Halal food

To be halal, animals have to be slaughtered in the right way. The act must be performed by a Muslim, who kills the animal while pronouncing the name of God.

The month of Ramadan

Ramadan is a special month for us because it was the month in which the words of the Qur'an were revealed to the Prophet Muhammad (pbuh). Muslims fast during the month of Ramadan, and this fast is one of the Pillars of Islam. That means that everyone must fast, except for some groups of people, such as women who are expecting a baby or those who are very sick.

The Ramadan fast

During Ramadan we eat less than usual, and eat only before sunrise and after sunset. We spend our days differently, too. We concentrate hard on our prayers and do not watch television; my father spends more time at the mosque. One special food we are allowed to eat during Ramadan is dates – we often have a snack of dates to break our daytime fast just after sunset.

◄ *People often eat falafels (made of ground chickpeas and spices) at the evening meal during Ramadan.*

21

My Favourite Festival
Jasmine's story

◀ My friend Sara gives me a hug at Eid.

One of my favourite times of the year is the festival of Eid. Eid marks the end of Ramadan, which is the month of fasting, and the beginning of the next month, Shawal. We celebrate Eid with good food and sometimes we get presents. Eid is also a time when people remember those who are poorer and less fortunate than themselves.

Prayers and donations
On the morning of Eid we get up extra early and go to prayers at a large stadium with thousands of other Muslims. Even though we give money to help the poor throughout the year, we remember the poor especially during Ramadan and Eid and give donations to charity.

Decorations
In some countries, people put up balloons and other decorations for Eid. Although people in America do not do this very much, I sometimes make little drawings on paper and stick them on the wall.

Eid celebrations

Eid begins when the new moon appears to signal the end of the fast of Ramadan. We celebrate Eid with a lovely meal. According to where we go for our meal, the food can be Malaysian, Pakistani or Middle Eastern. When we meet our friends during Eid we greet them with the phrase 'Eid Mubarak' ('Happy Eid'), and exchange lots of hugs and kisses. I sometimes exchange presents with my closest friends.

Jeffrey says:

At Eid I go to the mosque first thing in the morning with my grandfather, dad and uncle. Later we have a family breakfast with special curry and rice dishes. Afterwards we celebrate with friends, family and neighbours – Malaysians of all religions join in the celebrations and people give the children little green packets containing money.

▼ *These Muslims in Pakistan have just left the mosque after prayers on the first day of Eid. They are now buying colourful balloons to decorate their houses for the festival.*

Pilgrimage
Jasmine's story

▲ *I hope to go on the pilgrimage to Makka when I am older.*

Serish says:
My Grandma is one of the members of my family who has been on the pilgrimage to Makka. People like her who have made the pilgrimage are greatly respected.

The pilgrimage, or Hajj, to Makka is the fifth Pillar of Islam, and all Muslims hope to make the journey if they can afford it and if they are strong enough. The Hajj is a spiritual journey, following in the footsteps of the Prophet Abraham **and his wife Hagar.**

Prayers and rituals at Makka

On Hajj, pilgrims pray, perform special rituals and spend time in quiet reflection. The rituals take place in the Sacred Mosque at Makka, and at places nearby, such as Mina and Arafat. At Makka, people make for the Sacred Mosque where the Ka'aba is sited. The Ka'aba is a stone building put up by the Prophet Abraham and rebuilt by the Prophet Muhammad (pbuh). The pilgrims walk around the Ka'aba seven times counterclockwise, saying a special prayer as they go.

At Arafat and Mina

At Mount Arafat, where the Prophet Muhammad (pbuh) gave his last sermon, the pilgrims ask God for forgiveness. The pilgrims also spend time at the town of Mina, where the Prophet Abraham and his son Ismael came when God tested Abraham by asking him if he would sacrifice his son.

Looking forward to the journey

It must be awesome to be with millions of people all doing the same things and I hope to go on the pilgrimage when I am old enough. I will probably go with my mom and friends when I am about 15 years old.

Jeffrey says:
The Prophet Muhammad (pbuh) was born in Makka. He was a smart and brave man who never gave up his belief in Islam, even when faced with **idol**-worshippers and non-believers who thought he was crazy.

▼ *Muslims on Hajj go to the Sacred Mosque in Makka. At the centre of the mosque courtyard is the building known as the Ka'aba, around which the pilgrims walk.*

A New Baby
Serish's story

When a new baby is born into a Muslim family, everyone is pleased, because we believe that children are a gift from God. We carry out several ceremonies to mark the very special time when a new baby is born.

Welcoming the child

When the child is born, the father whispers the Adhan, or call to prayer, into his or her ear. This tells the child that he or she is a Muslim and welcomes the baby into the Islamic community. In some families, the Shahada, the Islamic profession of faith (see page 8) is whispered into the baby's ear.

▲ I am holding my baby brother Ammar.

Mohammad says:
When a new baby arrives, it is a happy time. The parents give thanks to God for the gift of a new member of the family.

Shaving the head

Soon after the birth, the baby's hair is shaved off. The reason for doing this is to ensure that the child is clean after it has been in its mother's womb. The parents then take the hair and weigh it. They give an equivalent amount of gold or silver to the poor. This is a way of giving thanks for the new child while also helping others.

Jasmine says:
In America, the Shahada, or Profession of Faith, is whispered into the new baby's ear. We do not follow the custom of shaving the baby's hair as is done in some other Muslim cultures.

Sacrifices

If the baby is a boy, he is circumcised when he is seven days old. Another birth custom, also on the seventh day of the child's life, is to make a sacrifice of two lambs when a boy is born and one lamb if the child is a girl. The family give the meat to relatives and the poor.

◄ *This is my father with me and my baby brother.*

Glossary

Abraham The Ancient ancestor of the people of the Middle East.

Adhan The call to prayer, made by the muezzin from the mosque about 15 minutes before prayer is due to begin.

circumcise To remove part of the foreskin of a boy's penis.

community A group of people who live in the same region or who have something, such as their religious beliefs, in common.

Eid (also 'Id, or 'Id al-Fitr) The festival that marks the end of the fast of Ramadan; there is a special festival prayer, people give alms to the poor, and there is a feast.

Hajj The pilgrimage to the holy city of Makka; Hajj is one of the Pillars of Islam.

halal What is lawful or permitted, especially food that Muslims are allowed to eat.

haram What is forbidden or restricted, especially food that Muslims are not allowed to eat, but also actions that are not permitted in Islamic law.

idol A picture or statue of a god used as an object of worship.

Imam The person who leads prayers at a mosque, or who acts as the leader of a particular Muslim community.

Ka'aba The large stone structure covered in black cloth that stands in the middle of the Grand Mosque at Makka. The Ka'aba was said to have been built by Adam, the first man, and rebuilt by Abraham and others, and so is the most ancient structure dedicated to the worship of God.

mahr The bride-price or gift given by a groom to his wife when they marry.

mosque The building where Muslims come together for prayers.

muezzin The person who makes the call to prayer from the mosque.

pbuh 'peace be upon him' Words often said by Muslims as a mark of respect and reverence after uttering the name of the prophet Muhammad (pbuh).

persecute To harass or hurt a person, especially for their beliefs.

Abraham The Ancient ancestor of the people of the Middle East.

Adhan The call to prayer, made by the muezzin from the mosque about 15 minutes before prayer is due to begin.

circumcise To remove part of the foreskin of a boy's penis.

community A group of people who live in the same region or who have something, such as their religious beliefs, in common.

Eid (also 'Id, or 'Id al-Fitr) The festival that marks the end of the fast of Ramadan; there is a special festival prayer, people give alms to the poor, and there is a feast.

Hajj The pilgrimage to the holy city of Makka; Hajj is one of the Pillars of Islam.

halal What is lawful or permitted, especially food that Muslims are allowed to eat.

haram What is forbidden or restricted, especially food that Muslims are not allowed to eat, but also actions that are not permitted in Islamic law.

idol A picture or statue of a god used as objects of worship.

Further Information

Websites
BBC Religion and Ethics
www.bbc.co.uk/religion/religions/islam

Religion Facts
www.religionfacts.com/islam

How Muslims Pray and What They Say
www.howmuslimspray.com

Islamia
www.islamia.com

The Muslim Year

The Muslim Year is based on a lunar calendar of 12 months, each of which has either 29 or 30 days. The Muslim year therefore has a year of 354 or 355 days, ten days shorter than the Western or Gregorian year in use in most parts of the world, so the Islamic months and festivals occur on different Gregorian dates each year. The Gregorian dates on which Islamic holidays and festivals occur can additionally vary, because each Islamic month only begins when the new Moon is actually seen. Although Muslims may use the Gregorian calendar for business or other purposes, they use the Islamic calendar for religious purposes.

Western equivalents of important Islamic holy days in 2008

Ra's al-'Am	Jan 10, 2008
Ashura	Jan 19, 2008
Mawlid an-Nabi	Mar 20, 2008
Ramadan begins	Sep 2, 2008
Eid	Oct 2, 2008
Dhu l-Hijjah begins	Nov 30, 2008
Eid al-Adha	Dec 9, 2008

The Muslim year contains several festivals that mark special events in the history of Islam and the life of the Prophet Muhammad (pbuh). These festivals are celebrated in different ways in different parts of the world. There are also festivals and parts of the year connected to the Pillars of Islam. These parts of the calendar, the months of Ramadan and Dhu l-Hijjah, are marked in a similar way throughout the Muslim community, with fasting in Ramadan and pilgrimage in Dhu l-Hijjah.

Ra's al-'Am

The Islamic New Year, Ra's al-'Am, is on the first day of the month of Muharram. It marks the date of the Hijra, Muhammad's (pbuh) departure from Makka to the city of Medina in the year CE 622.

Ashura

The festival of Ashura is especially important to the Shi'a Muslims. It is a solemn time that commemorates the death in CE 680 of Hussayn, a pious and brave Imam, who was Muhammad's (pbuh) grandson. He gave his life in a battle defending Islam against the unjust rulers of Iraq. In some places there are processions, and plays re-enacting Hussayn's death are performed.

Mawlid an-Nabi

The birthday of the Prophet Muhammad (pbuh) is celebrated on the 12th day of the month of Rabi' al-Awwal (The first spring). People celebrate the Prophet's birth and life, and in Muslim countries the day is a public holiday.

Ramadan

During this month, Muslims fast during the hours of daylight. The fast during Ramadan is one of the Pillars of Islam (see page 5).

Eid

The first day of the month of Shawwal marks the end of the fasting of Ramadan. This festival, known as Eid al-Fitr, or simply Eid, is celebrated with a prayer, and people also share a special meal and give alms to the poor.

Dhu l-Hijjah

This month is the time when the pilgrimage to the city of Makka (see pages 24–25) takes place.

Eid al-Adha

This is a four-day festival that takes place after the great pilgrimage to Makka. People sacrifice animals and give the meat to the poor.

Index